THE MAGIC QUESTION

How to Get What You Want in Half the Time

*One simple daily technique to change your life,
get unstuck, attract wealth, be more creative,
program optimism, and live your life
with exuberant happiness.*

Bart A. Baggett

ISBN: 1-882929-18-7
ISBN-13: 978-1-882929-18-4

Published by Empresse Publishing
www.empressepublishing.com

www.bartbaggett.com

Other books and programs by Bart A. Baggett

Success Secrets of the Rich and Happy: How to Design Your Life with Financial and Emotional Abundance.

....

Unstoppable You! How to have the emotional state of happiness, confidence, and live with purpose .

....

The Grapho-Deck:
Learn Handwriting Analysis in 10 Minutes A Day

....

Change Your Handwriting, Change Your Life Workbook (Kids and Adults Version)

....

Unstoppable Confidence Guided Meditation

....

Fearless Living - Overcome Self Consciousness & Fear of Rejection Guided Meditation

....

Handwriting Analysis 101: Introduction to the Basic Personality Traits In Handwriting.

....

Handwriting Analysis Certification Level Home Study Course for Personality Profiling & Transformation

....

Handwriting Analysis:
Secrets of Love and Fulfilling Relationships

Table of Contents

READ THIS FIRST

Many readers enjoy hearing their favorite books in audio format. So, to say thanks for purchasing this book, I'd like to give you the audiobook 100% FREE!

Download here:
http://bartbaggett.com/books/magicquestion.html

**Scan this code with your phone
and download the audiobook
100% FREE!**

1 Introduction

The Magic Question is based on one powerful mental technique that I discovered over two decades ago. I have been using it and refining the process for my own personal growth ever since.

This single process has helped me achieve numerous business successes, meet influential people, have adventures in foreign lands, and find happiness and joy in each moment, which otherwise might have eluded me.

Now that I've fully come to understand how powerful this single technique is, I'd like to share it with you. I sincerely believe it will help you attract more opportunities for love, wealth, and adventure in a world where so many have lack and struggle. I have used it to get unstuck, make life decisions, and find creative answers which shifted the direction of my life in ways beyond words. If nothing else, using the Magic Question on a daily basis will help program optimism and provide a sense of hope, which might have been missing. In the best circumstances, it will engender a lifelong shift in your thinking, and will open doors to a more fulfilled life.

Furthermore, I have no doubt that any professional trainer, counselor, coach, or public speaker can begin to use this technique in live seminars and one-on-one counseling sessions right away. It is my hope that this technique will become as common as the idea of "Visualization" in the personal development field.

As far as I know, I was the first to use the terms "The Magic Question" in my seminars and workshops. The term "direction question" was coined by Rex Sykes in the 1990's and was probably the logical ancestry to this idea is it germinated in my brain for two decades. Feel free to teach it to your friends and family as they look for simple tools to change their thinking patterns.

I've intentionally kept this book concise so you can read it in one sitting. The strategies and ideas are clearly explained, easy to implement, and highly effective. You needn't take my word for how powerful this technique is. If you put it into practice for just 21 days, you'll prove it to yourself and the people around you.

How Brian's Magic Questions Turned His Finances Around

I'll tell you a quick story about my friend, Brian. A few years ago, he made some poor business decisions while experiencing an emotionally- draining divorce. Suddenly he found himself $50,000 in debt. Many people would have filed for bankruptcy, but Brian decided to take the high road and pay back his debt. Given his current income, it would have taken him 30 years to dig himself out of this financial hole.

Instead of complaining or giving up, he started with some key questions. He asked these questions of himself and those he respected. Here is the series he asked himself for weeks, before a plan came into view.

"How can I pay off this debt within three years?"

"What needs to happen for me to pay off this debt quickly and easily?"

"I wonder where I can earn extra money to pay this debt off even faster."

"How good will I feel when I am debt-free?"

What Brian was doing was challenging his unconscious mind to find solutions to his problem. Sure enough, Brian began attracting the right opportunities, and was smart enough to take action on them. He ended up getting job offers to travel the world editing high-end corporate videos. He did pay off those credit cards and loans within three years. Furthermore, the opportunities that came because he kept asking well-structured direction questions took him to a new level of career success and income. As a bonus, his integrity and strong work ethic took him to the far corners of the globe as part of his career. He has been using the same formula inside the Magic Question to transition from a video editor to a full-time fiction writer. This technique works. It is something you will use to solve problems, find solutions, and guide your mental state on a daily basis.

There is always an Option C

One of the most useful problem-solving techniques I've used over the past 30 years is a concept I now call "Option C". Before I explain how this works, let me tell you a story.

As I was writing the final chapter of this book, I found myself driving in Santa Monica, California, on a bright, sunny day. On the corner of Lincoln Boulevard and Ocean Park Avenue I sat waiting at a traffic light, observing a slightly out-of-shape homeless woman in her early 30s, digging through a garbage can. I was immediately overcome with sadness and compassion. Then, to my surprise, she picked up a Styrofoam cup and drank the remaining beverage with a straw. She grinned with a moment of pleasure and placed the empty cup back into the trashcan, replaced the lid, and wandered off. I imagine she was continuing her search for more food.

In that moment, I recalled a belief and concept that might be useful to you, the reader. I have a belief that people make the best decisions they can in any situation, given the choices they see in front of them.

Even given two terrible choices, people choose the lesser of two evils. I imagine that nice homeless woman was walking the streets, seeing a very limited number of options from which to feed herself. I speculate she was asking the question, "Does that trashcan have any food or drink?" Perhaps she was asking herself this morning, "Should I stand on the street and beg for money or dig through trashcans?"

What I wish I could have explained to her, and you, and the entire world, is the idea that, in any situation, no matter how dire, there is always an Option C.

Here is what I mean. In any tough decision, we often narrow down our choices to A or B. Should we pay rent or buy groceries? Should we buy a Mercedes or a Lexus? Should I go to Pepperdine or USC? Should I leave and get a divorce or stay? Should I rob a bank or be poor all my life? Should I invest in gold or silver? Should we move to Bel Air or Pacific Palisades?

We tend to narrow down our choices to two, and sweat out the details of the pros and cons of those two choices. Here is the most enlightening belief I have ever created for myself. Regardless of the content of your Option A and Option B decision, there is always an Option C.

The problem is that we simply don't see an Option C when we are focused on deciding between Options A and B.

What do you think would have happened if she had thought of an Option C, which netted her $50 a time? What if she walked up to every person in a nice car and said, "Excuse me, I've got a job interview tomorrow and don't have clean clothes or new dress to wear"? Could you help me buy a new dress so I can possibly get my life back together?" I can tell you know, if she had asked me that question, I would have handed her $20, $30, or even taken her shopping. Whether it was a lie or not, the frame of the conversation would have moved me to give a $20 bill, not a few quarters. That is the point. Many times in life, we settle for loose change when $20 bills are only inches away.

Clearly, she would have chosen to get $20 donations every time instead of eating from a garbage can. I've never been so destitute that I felt my only option was to beg on the street corner. But, I have to say the rejection and scorn they must feel on a daily basis must be heartbreaking. There are dozens of reasons that the hypothetical Option C is something she would never had really gone through with.

In situations that seem hopeless, it's very, very difficult to brainstorm an Option C solution. That's the point of this book. If you follow the structure of how to form a Magic Question, you will begin to see Option C, Option D, Option E, etc. If you find enough new options, one of them will fit your beliefs, abilities, and morals to move you to a new place of hope and action. Once people realize there are more than two options, they make better decisions, and their lives change in profound ways.

This book is not about giving you the answers to getting rich, fixing your marriage, losing weight, investing your money, or even being happier. This book is designed to show you a simple new "thought process", which will help you discover the many options you really do have which have been hidden from view. However, it would not surprise me if the results of your thinking differently were more health, wealth, and love.

The Power of The Magic Question Over Time

When I was 15 years old, my father took me to a sales seminar led by the legendary self-improvement guru Tom Hopkins. This world of seminars and training was a world I did not know even existed. It was like a space alien coming to America and landing at midfield of the Super Bowl. This exists? Why? What's going on? How fun!

I remember asking myself this question, "How can I be on that stage one day?" That simple question gave me a direction in life that lasts to this very day. Over time and lots of work, I found myself on speaking on stages from Chicago, USA to Mumbai, India, training people on the ideas of improving their life.

When I was 21, I asked myself this question, "How can I become a published author by the age of 24?" Trust me, becoming a published author was a much bigger mountain to climb in the 1990s than it is in today's self-publishing world of Amazon.com. Sure enough, a few days before I turned 24, my first box of freshly-printed books arrived at my house and I sat proudly, knowing I was now in the very elite club of "published authors".

A few years before that magical moment of entering the world of publishing, I found myself working at a "real job" in the emerging city of Las Vegas. I was surrounded by people whose only question about career and money was "How can I make more money per hour?" The only options they saw for themselves were A) Stay at the hotel I'm at and B) Get a job at a different hotel.

That seemed to me to be a very limiting set of choices. It was then that I started asking questions like, "How can I own my own business and have freedom?" I asked myself, "What business can I start that will provide residual income for the rest of my life?" I continued to seek out and study people like Jay Abraham, who charged $5,000 for a box of cassette tapes. What was he doing differently that I could learn from? I read books by a guy named Stuart Wilde, whose fans happily travelled halfway around the world, and paid him thousands of dollars to spend a weekend learning from his wisdom. I read books by Donald Trump, and discovered that there is an entire world of men and woman who deal in billions of dollars per transaction. That was a world I wanted to play in... not the world where people worried about how much a customer tipped them on a Saturday night.

I was determined to find the Option C. I didn't know what Option C looked like, but I had a belief it DID exist, and I was going to find it.

Fast forward just 12 years later in Beverly Hills, California. I found myself sitting in the office with the very famous and very kind Merv Griffin. At this point, Merv Griffin was a billionaire. He was the same guy I had read about 15 years earlier inside those Donald Trump books, who went head-to-head with Mr. Trump on some real estate deals. Here I was sitting face-to-face with a living legend.

Merv was producing a television show for which he was hand-picking the stars. There was a role for a handwriting expert and I had established myself as a reliable expert in that field. But, before we got down to the business of television, he just wanted to visit. He shared a few amazing stories about his life during and after his famous talk show, "The Merv Griffin Show" (On air from 1962-1986). He was more magnanimous and kind than you can imagine.

He asked me to walk around his office and analyze the signatures on all the signed photographs on his wall. After analyzing the handwriting of famous movie stars, titans of industry, and ex-presidents, I came upon the writing of Nancy Reagan. I gave the analysis with the precision and accuracy I had become famous for. He laughed, "Yep. That's Nancy! You nailed it. She can be all that and more." He then told me about the amazing golden retriever which had been keeping us company during the entire meeting. He said, "By the way, Nancy and Ron have been friends of mine for 30 years. In fact, she gave me my dog. She is still a dear friend."

We went on to make that TV pilot. Working with Merv Griffin was a major catalyst in my interest in the TV and film business. In the years since that meeting, Merv passed away, to the sadness of everyone who knew him.

The point I want to leave you with is this: How did a 22-year-old kid in a dead-end job in Las Vegas end up working with one of the most famous billionaires on the planet just a dozen years later? It was simple... I asked better questions. Thus, I found better answers than those who never asked those questions in the first place.

How to Best Learn From This Book

In the final chapter of the book, I've included dozens of "Magic Questions" which might fit your particular life situation. I've done the work for you. Just choose your question for the day, and let your unconscious mind do all the work.

However, if you were to skip ahead to choose the one question that resonates with you without reading the book, you wouldn't know how to use the question effectively, and the results would be less pronounced than if you read the book cover to cover.

As a wise man once said, "Give a man a fish and feed him for a day. Teach a man to fish and feed him for a lifetime."

If you invest just a little time in learning the process and reasons behind the seemingly magic question, you will begin to create your own, real-time, in hundreds of situations for the rest of your life... practically on autopilot.

Understanding how your brain sorts information is the key to this process. Once you fully grasp the fundamental concepts, you will be able to create your own customized Magic Questions, and use this simple language tool to become a better parent, spouse, employee, manager, or anything else... and naturally become happier as you do it.

Asking Questions

Can You Turn Outdated Goal-Setting Into An Effective Magic Question?

Since Napoleon Hill first penned his classic book in 1937, it has been commonplace to use goal-setting and affirmations to help shift your mindset. This book is different. For example, traditional self-help books would encourage you to say things like, "I'm definitely going to make $100,000 next year." This book is suggesting there is a better way, using Magic Questions.

What if you turned these desires and goals into questions? What if it was twice as effective and twice as useful to ask yourself the following:

- "How is it that I'm going to make $100,000 next year?"

- "What am I going to produce that will create the value to earn me $100,000?"

- "How easy would it be to earn $100,000 this year?"

- "How much fun can I have while earning lots of money?"

These types of well-crafted questions actually pull your unconscious mind in a specific, creative direction. The great thing about direction questions is that they leapfrog your current belief systems, and propel you forward to finding solutions that would have previously gone unnoticed. These are only a few samples of what is a very specific structure I will call the Magic Question.

How I Became a B-Movie Action Hero

Now, most of my readers and fans know me around the world as an author, motivational speaker, and handwriting expert. What many people don't know is that I created a fun, part-time career for myself in the film business... in my spare time, using the Magic Question technique... and effort.

In 2012, I was living in Los Angeles, and invested some of my free time in the film and TV business. Although I had already been in a few films as an actor, and a few national TV commercials, I didn't have a flow of offers to play bigger roles. In all honesty, I was loving every minute of every role. However, I had decided making movies was more fun than TV or radio shows, so I decided to focus my energy just on feature films. I wrote out one question, which I looked at every morning as I brushed my teeth. The question was, "How can I easily get myself hired to act in at least two feature films a year?"

I was attending the birthday part of my manager, Phil Brock, and struck up a casual conversation with an actor friend of mine, named Gerald Webb, who was working in casting for a very successful low-budget film company. He asked if I had a current passport. "Of course; I can leave tomorrow. Where do you want me to go?" He said there was a slight possibility he could get me a major role in a thriller, shooting in the Bahamas starting in five days... assuming I could get to the island by Sunday. Done.

Five days later, I was walking along a white, sandy beach on the island of Eleuthera, filming a fight scene for the science-fiction movie *Shark Week*. No audition. No callback. No long meeting with producers.

It was one of the most interesting and fun times of my life. Unfortunately, as in most low-budget suspense shark thrillers, my character was eaten by a shark in Scene 3. Just for the record, in movies, I've died by shark attack, exploding van hit by a helicopter in *Airline Disaster,* the famous whale, Moby Dick, eating my submarine in *Moby Dick 2010*, and an exploding green car in the Seth Rogan movie, *Green Hornet*. I even get to live in a few movies. Ha. Life is such a hoot.

I asked the right questions. I expected opportunities. I looked for people who could help me. I looked for people I could help. I saw it and took action. Thoughts and intentions are powerful things. The secret lies in your ability to control the voice in your head, and ask better questions. I never asked questions like, "Why can't I get more movies? Why don't producers cast me more? Why not me?" Those questions are totally un-empowering and do not lead to useful outcomes.

2 Test Your Brain

A Fun Game to Test Your Brain

Before we get into the mental science upon which this book is based, let's have some fun.

Over the next few pages, I've provided a few images I'd like you to take a look at for just 10 seconds.

You will get more benefit if you play along and have fun with it.

So, the rules are simple. First, make sure to read the question twice so you are absolutely sure you understand what you are being asked to look for in each image. Once you are ready, flip the page and give yourself just 10 seconds to read the question. Then, flip to the next page to read the paragraph which follows. After the first image, you are welcome to go back to the question and reflect on how well your brain took in the information in the short, 10-second game.

Ready? Go.

Look at the following image and find the shape of the vase. In 10 seconds, turn the page.

▶ ▶ ▶   Next Page   ▶ ▶ ▶

So, did you see a vase, or two faces?

Look back at the image, both are correct answers. The white part forms the vase, the black part forms two faces looking at each other.

Image 2:

Look at the following image and count the number of pillars which are holding up the roof in the drawing. In 10 seconds, turn the page.

So, how many pillars did you see? Now without looking at the image again... answer a second question: How many people are in the picture?

3, 4, 1, 0, 10?

If you got the number of pillars correct, congratulations. Your brain can find what it is looking for quickly. However, if you did not remember seeing the eight people, you are completely normal. How many sets of bars on the windows? Four. How many people are standing on the top floor? One.

By the way, I counted 16 pillars. However, that question is not as relevant to the topic of this book as the subsequent questions.

Let's do one more graphic game before we get into the meat of this book. This image represents the type of game I have had audiences do from London to Mumbai, with amazing "Ah Ha" results every time.

Look at the following photograph and count the number of items that are the color red. In 10 seconds, turn the page.

Good. Thanks for playing.

Now, without looking at the image of the classroom again, take a few moments and write down exactly how many items in the classroom are black. Go ahead, take a minute and write down your answer before you look at the image again.

If you are like most of my audiences, you saw the red items (shirts, jackets, paper, folders, etc.), but totally under-counted the black items. The black items include the spotlights, speakers, tele-prompters, chairs, and lots of blouses and sweaters.

This simple game illustrates the power of the mind and the power of the direction question better than I could ever do explaining this with just words.

By the way, in live seminars, this game is played with colors in a hotel room. The audience is always totally amazed by the number of items which were literally sitting right in front of them that they missed. Pens, coffee cups, the shirt on their back. It's all about reprogramming your mind to notice and take inventory of the things your unconscious mind has decided weren't important enough to bring to your attention.

3 The Discovery

How I Discovered the Magic Question Technique.

The first time I was ever exposed to this general idea was at a Tony Robbins seminar in 1989. I didn't have much money, but really loved attending live, personal-development seminars. I asked myself the question, "How can I attend Tony's seminars for free?" Naturally, the answer came to me when a friend said I could volunteer as a staff member and attend for free. I was stoked. Tony said many brilliant things that weekend. One particularly interesting quote stuck with me. He said, "The quality of your life is the quality of your questions."

However, it was easy to skip over the idea as just a footnote or a concept. I didn't have a tangible system to make that mental habit a usable tactic to use day in and day out. This book contains that system.

Over the next decade, I attended dozens of seminars and read hundreds of books on personal development. I discovered hundreds of good ideas regarding the process of how your brain thinks.

It wasn't until 1996 that I saw a refined and elegant easy-to-follow technique which changed this concept into a usable application. This application of the idea was the basis of what I now call "The Magic Question".

In seminars, I sometimes refer to this as a "Direction Question".

This term is probably more accurate, because it isn't really magic; it's brain science, which pushes your mind in the direction of what you want. However, people love magic and it sounds catchy.

I have to give thanks to one of my NLP trainers, Rex Sykes, for his part in inspiring the Magic Question concept. During a two-week NLP Certification Program, Rex asked (demanded) that we start each day by playing a game he called "Good & New". It sounds pretty simple, until you do it two to three times a day, for two weeks straight.

He had us stand in a circle, and one person would throw you the rubber ball as they would state something in their life that was both good and new.

The mental process is simply to ask yourself, "What's good and what's new?" Your brain starts searching for answers and out come things like "My shoes. Breakfast. The flowers in the garden. My friend, Johnny, etc."

This is pretty easy the first few days. However, one of the rules of the game is that you can't use the same answer someone has already given, so you have to find fresh things which are good and new.

What resulted was an increase in time between asking the question, "What's good and new?" and the person's answer. The brain took longer to find an answer that fit the criteria.

The game became more difficult and lasted longer because the easy answers were "off the board". Our brains had to really dig deep to find a new answer.

This was the key.

We began finding things that our subconscious had already sorted out, and locating solutions that existed, but were not at our "top of mind" awareness.

The end result was that everyone in the seminar became happier, and experienced the emotion of optimism. If you were to summarize the new belief that Rex programmed, it might be articulated as "Every day brings something good and new."

That's a powerful experience. We had intentionally programmed in ourselves a brand-new belief that automatically creates optimism in us the moment we wake up.

At that moment, I realized that I had discovered a quick, daily procedure I could use to reprogram my mind, belief systems, and even "shortcut" the process-setting goals and achieving them.

In the context of family and children, I used to play this game while driving, in order to turn a grumpy child into an optimist. I taught this simple game to a single mom friend of mine in Los Angeles, who had two very smart and rambunctious pre-teens.

While pre-teens and teenagers can be a bit defiant when asked to play a word game, once they got into playing the game, the kids went from finding everything wrong in the world to finding what was good and new. The car rides became much more pleasant for their mom, me and, of course, the siblings argued less in the back seat.

This is a great tip for any parent. Teach your kids to ask "Magic Questions", which focus on what they want, instead of what they don't want. Try the "Good & New Game" next time you pick your kids up from school.

While the question of "Good & New" is just one example of an empowering Magic Question, it is by no means the **one question** which will supercharge your career, transform your finances, attract love into your life, or overcome a health issue.

In the field of NLP (Neuro-Lingustic Programming), they called this shifting from a "problem frame" to an "outcome frame". Whether or not you believe a situation to be good or bad, the idea that you can find positive outcomes even in bad situations is a huge mental shift.

Change the inner voice from "Why don't kids like me?" to the question, "What things do kids like about me?"

Change the inner voice from, "Why do I always screw everything up?" to this question, "What things have I done very well this past year?"

The Magic Question, which you will use to transform your life in about 21 days, is probably already written for you in the last chapter, or you will write it all by yourself before you complete this book.

I'll tell you a quick story of how this process helped me double my income in just a few months.

Back in 1997, I had found quite a bit of success appearing on morning radio shows as a guest. Sometimes I was in-studio, talking about my books, or I was sitting at home, talking on the telephone to a radio host 1,000 miles away.

After about 100 interviews, it occurred to me that getting on radio shows was one of the cheapest and most fun marketing techniques I've ever experienced to get new customers, get my message out, and have a ton of fun.

So, I wrote down these words on a note card and set it on my desk for the next month. The card just had one sentence, "How can I get on three radio shows a week?"

That question sparked a series of meetings, conferences, and phone calls that has had profound results in my business.

Within a few months, I had met and hired a full-time "radio-booking agent", with no money out of my pocket (paid a percentage of sales), and attended a Morning Show Radio Host Bootcamp (which I did not know even existed). At that event, I met hundreds of morning show hosts in one location and forged relationships that still result in my being invited

on the air to this day. Very quickly, I started appearing on
two to four shows a week… and selling thousands of dollars'
worth of self-help products to audiences.

In 1999, I appeared on the Howard Stern Show and sold
$30,000 worth of books/CDs in my 30-minute appearance.
By 2003, I had appeared on over 1,500 radio shows and even
was offered to host my own show by CBS's FM talk station
105.3. This was a boom for my business and celebrity status.
It started because I asked myself one specific, powerful,
direction question.

Now, *let me explain to your conscious mind* why this works
like magic. It is all rooted in neuroscience and psychology…

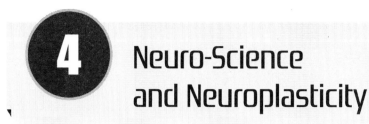

4 Neuro-Science and Neuroplasticity

Neuro-Science and Neuroplasticity

Have you ever studied Quantum Physics?

It's a very deep subject, and it's pretty complicated, actually. There's a great movie called *What the Bleep Do We Know?* Go rent it if you want to get a great snapshot of this discipline and be entertained at the same time.

Fantastic movie. They interviewed many scholars, physicists, and scientists. And I'll tell you, physicists are not comedians. It's hard to interview a physicist and compel him/her to be funny, but they are very interesting. I can't imagine being married to one.

What they found out was that, by using an ultra-powerful microscope, a sub-atomic microscope, they were tracking movements of atoms through the universe. Which is amazing and it's so small that we can barely even perceive it; not with our own eyes, but barely with modern microscopes.

Sub-Atomic Particles

What they found was the molecule actually changed direction as a direct result of the observer's presence. Now, that's crazy, right? But a particle at a sub-atomic level changes direction in direct proportion to whether or not there's a consciousness observing it.

That's amazing! So, does that mean that your thoughts and your intentions can actually change physical matter? That's pretty profound. Most of us think that we have to take action to get a result. I have to physically move the universe in order to get a result. That's the way we tend to think: I have to go to work, I have to work hard, I have to get married... Actually! From a physics perspective, not just "woo-woo" meditation, hang out in India with my guru, "waa waa waa waa" (mimicking sitar sounds).

I'm not making fun; I actually like meditation so much, but they knew something a hundred years ago that physicists have now proven. Thoughts, in a certain sequence, actually manifest reality. And now it's proven, like, on a physical level. We are talking about something changeable, movable, and moldable about your brain that can be physically changed. (I talk more about this in Chapter 16 of my book *Success Secrets of the Rich and Happy*.)

I love reading and I'm also very creative. Most of what I teach is an amalgamation of my personal experience and other people's work, proven and tested for decades.

And so I'm not asking you to be a master trainer in hypnosis or in NLP (Neuro Linguistic Programming). I'm asking you to take some of the tools that are most useful, and apply them to your own life.

Success Tip: Once you've applied them to your own life, you can teach this simple technique to your friends and family. First, you need to experience the power of the Magic Questions first-hand.

It's very difficult to share something that you're not doing. If you've been divorced fifteen times, it's very difficult for you to be a love coach. Maybe a divorce coach, but not a love coach.

And that's the key. How can you turn even the most emotionally-painful situation into something happy and joyful? Well, it all starts with a better question.

One guy in Japan turned the most painful event in some people's lives into a fun and playful ceremony to provide closure and hope. Hiroki Terai started a business based around the idea of a "divorce ceremony".

Since starting the business in Tokyo, business is booming. Many people are obviously asking the question, "How can I get a divorce without all the fighting and suffering?" The divorce ceremony was the answer.

According to the New York Times, here is the question which turned Hiroki Terai into Tokyo's #1 Divorce Planner. "Ever since I was little, I wondered, if you have a wedding ceremony, why not have one to mark your divorce?" he explained to me with a smile.

Well, linguistically, that exact question falls short of the perfect Magic Question, but the interview was probably translated from Japanese. The real question, which I think drove him to start this business, was "How can turn a divorce into a positive, life-changing event?"

Now, he sells yellow "Divorce Dresses", which are designed to look more attractive when the ex-wife walks away. (Neckline plunges in the back.)

They have a smashing of the ring ceremony where the crushed ring is inserted into a three-foot ceramic frog's mouth. In Japan, the frog symbolizes a return or a time to find opportunities in transition. Isn't that appropriate for focusing on what's good about the divorce?

Isn't that fantastic? It costs about $600 for a divorce ceremony. I don't know how what a divorce should cost in Japan... but that sounds like a bargain to me.

So let's start exploring why magic questions are so powerful, with a little bit of scientific information about how your brain really works.

5 Thoughts and Memories

According to research, we can keep about seven things in our head consciously. In fact, in America, phone numbers were seven digits for many years.

Because we tend to remember seven digits, when you get to 10 or 12 or 14, you have to break them into smaller chunks. So if we remember phone numbers in 3, 4, 5, we can remember strings of numbers.

Which list of numbers is easier to remember?

15557874567

or

1-555-787-4567

So we can hold focus on only about seven things consciously at any given time.

Functions like your heartbeat, the air temperature, and the position of your feet are only part of your waking awareness when you need to know about it. Otherwise, it's all on autopilot.

So, because of the power of your unconscious mind to monitor all these things, it helps you focus on important things. This is a very useful feature of your mind.

The problem is if you keep only consciously seeing the seven things you've noticed in the past, you're going miss the 8th, 9th, and 10th things that might change your life.

So what you have to do is tell your mind to look for something new and different, instead of what you already know about.

The Magic Question is the shortcut to doing just that.

For instance, we would notice if a real-life monster showed up in right now, right? We would notice that because it's big, ugly, and scary. If a small lizard was crawling around the floor, we may not notice.

However, what would happen if I placed a big advertisement that said, "I will give you a million dollars for every lizard you bring me tomorrow!"

How many people would probably notice some lizards?

The whole world would be looking for lizards! And if a monster showed up, you may ignore the monster and go look for the lizard. Right? Look at the power of intention on that! Once you train your brain to look for what you really want, you can get it in half the time or even less.

6 R.A.S.

**Hijacking Your Brain For Wealth and Happiness:
Reticular Activator System**

In order to understand why the magic question works so well, it helps to understand how your brain really works. However, you can do a quick search on Google and be immediately overwhelmed with the deeply technical, medical, and biochemical explanations relating to the brains functionality, hormones, sleep patterns, and details about the required chemicals of your neuro-pathways.

My purpose is to simplify this knowledge, and extract the relevant information which you can apply to your life, today. If you do want to read the medical research, please refer to the footnotes at the end of this chapter.

'Hijack' is an interesting term, because what you are doing is a positive hijacking of your brain's attention span. Think of it as re-routing a plane to a new destination, if the word 'hijack' holds negative connotations.

One of the most interesting areas of brain research came when they discovered and labeled an area of the brain commonly called the R.A.S. (Reticular Activation System)

The R.A.S. is not one nerve cluster or organ. It's an area where dozens of neuron pathways intersect with various functions. Think of it like a telephone switchboard where only the most important calls are allowed to get through to the CEO of the company. Other, less urgent calls are sent to the department heads and other staff. All the calls get handled, but not directly by the CEO.

Your conscious mind is the CEO in this metaphor. Your unconscious is the rest of your staff, managers, and blue-collar workers who diligently work day after day. You often are happy to see the trash can empty, but you didn't really see who emptied it. You are happy to realize the water in your sink runs perfectly, but you don't exactly know who is responsible for making that happen.

Your internal R.A.S is that project coordinator that delegates all the functions from fatigue, heartbeat, temperature, and pain. It decides what grabs your conscious attention... all based on what you have, in the past, deemed important and relevant.

This is where you must hijack the system to program new instructions to allow data, which was previously deemed as not important, to become critically important.

Here is how author Marilee B. Sprenger explains the RAS in her book, *The Leadership Brain for Dummies*:

"The *reticular activating system* (RAS) is the portal through which nearly all information enters the brain. (Smells are the exception; they go directly into your brain's emotional area.) The RAS filters the incoming information and affects what you pay attention to, how aroused you are, and what is not going to get access to all three pounds of your brain.

For survival's sake, your RAS responds to your name, anything that threatens your survival, and information that you need immediately. For instance, if you're looking for a computer file that you're sure you placed on your desk, your RAS alerts your brain to search for the name of the file — Andrews vs. State of Illinois, say — or focus on one word in the filename to help you find it.

The RAS also responds to novelty. You notice anything new and different."

From a scientist's view, this is correct. However, most brain scientists would argue that the most important part of the RAS system is controlling your sleep and brainwave patterns. While this is very simplistic, it is important to realize that if you are totally asleep, then you are not alert, not learning, and not making conscious decisions.

Likewise, the RAS is responsible for pulling you out of your nighttime slumber and waking you up. That is what the magic question can do for your life; wake you up to the new and unnoticed possibilities all around you.

I particularly like what he says about how he thinks daydreaming is a version of self-talk. Naturally, it is self-talk with images for many of us. However, after you read Brad's quote, I will explain why auditory messages (self-talk and external noise) are the most directly path to overriding and manipulating your own RAS system. This is another secret why the magic question works so well if you just ask the question in your own natural voice.

Here is what leadership consultant, **Brad Worthley, says about the RAS system.**

"In short, it is the attention center of the brain, and it is the switch that turns your brain on and off. When functioning properly, it provides the connections that are needed for the processing and learning of information, plus the ability to stay focused on the correct task."

"The Reticular Activating System is best known as a filter, because it sorts out what is important information that needs to be paid attention to and what is unimportant and can be ignored. Without this filter, we would all be over-stimulated and distracted by noises from our environment around us. As an example, let's just say you were a mother who has a baby sleeping in the next room, and you live right next to a busy airport with lots of loud noise from jets taking off and landing. Despite the constant roar of the jets and other noise, you will hear your baby if it makes even the smallest noise in the next room. The Reticular Activating System filters out the airport noise, which is unimportant to you, and keeps you focused on your baby, which is the most important thing to you. The Reticular Activating System is like a filter between your conscious mind and your subconscious mind. It takes instructions from your conscious mind (like "*I need to hear my baby*") and passes it on to your subconscious mind, which becomes diligent and alert to your request."

In the world of learning, the Reticular Activating System is like a switch in your head that turns on and off based on how much telling tension or self-talk you have going on inside your head. If the switch is open, you can retain information easily, and if the switch is closed, you cannot. If you are sitting in a seminar, bored because the person speaking is not engaging enough (your brain is not stimulated enough), your Reticular Activating System will turn off and treat the person as irritating background noise, just like the noisy airport in the previous example. We will still see the person speaking and hear their voice, but we will not retain the information."

I will give you a couple of examples of how the Reticular Activating System may have impacted you.

Remember sitting in a classroom for an hour? You are almost certain the teacher was there, because you could see them walking around and you could hear their voice, even though you are not certain about the message. You thought you were listening because you could see them and hear their voice. However, at the end of the class you got up, walked out the door and you have very little, if any, memory about what you learned. That is because, if the teacher was not engaging enough to you, you disengaged and you began to daydream. You went to a happy place and thought about your upcoming date this weekend, your new car, or about an idea you had for a company you would like to start someday. Daydreaming is self-talk, which shuts the Reticular Activating System off and makes it difficult for you to retain what the teacher is saying."

"I will give you another example. Have you ever driven down a freeway on a sunny afternoon, daydreaming until you awaken suddenly after five minutes, realizing that you missed your exit? You don't remember cars passing you or if you passed other cars, and you don't remember what was on the radio. It should terrify you that you are a 3,000-pound missile flying down the freeway at 60 miles an hour, and you have no memory of the last five minutes of your drive. How can that possibly be? It's because daydreaming is self-talk, which shuts down the Reticular Activating System and keeps you from remembering.

Staying present is the most important part of keeping the Reticular Activating System open and absorbing what is being said."

Why Your Own Voice is so Darn Effective.

There is a scientific reason the magic question can be more effective than dream boards, visualization, affirmations, or even goal-planning. The reason is simple. Your RAS responds better to auditory commands than to other options. That means that words and sounds are particularly effective at breaking through the RAS radar and getting your attention.

I do believe that setting goals once a year is a useful exercise. I even have seen first-hand the power of making a "dream board", with imagery of what you want. It can be useful and even tons of fun to make it and look at it every day.

I once met a woman who said she had over 100 sticky notes scattered around her house with positive affirmations written on them. She was disappointed that her life was not improving.

While dreams boards and handwritten sticky notes of affirmations can be useful and sometimes effective, they lose their effectiveness over time. Your RAS begins to ignore these items and focuses on the most important five to seven points of awareness that are most relevant to today's task. This is why the magic question is so effective. You are talking to yourself daily. You are creating a new auditory channel each time you read the question aloud. The magic question grabs your attention and moves your focus to this question. If only for a moment, your brain focuses on this. It's not magic; it's brain science.

We Can Thank Sleeping Cats for This.

An article published in 1952 in the *AMA Archives of Neurology and Psychiatry* explains how a researcher named Dr. Magoun proved that the RAS system was a holistic system, not just a single cluster of nerves located in just one area of the brain. He attached a series EEG electrodes and stimuli blockers to the brains of sleeping cats.

He discovered that even when blocking the traditional areas of the brain from communication, external sounds were very effective at waking the cat from a deep sleep. This indicated to him that this RAS system can bypasses traditional mid-brain neuropathways. Sound could still get through, even when the mid-brain communication was blocked.

You have probably been woken up from a deep sleep by loud noise in the middle of the night. This is because your ears never really turn off. The RAS system just sorts the data, and only communicates what is relevant or dangerous. Your RAS system is always on, even when you sleep.

Essentially, external sound gets to the brain... no matter what. This seems logical, as even a sleeping cat has his ears turned on to listen for danger.

It is said the RAS system still functions while under hypnosis, during surgery with anesthesia, or totally asleep. This is a very useful defense mechanism. The auditory system records everything, even if you can't remember hearing it.

What this tells me is that when you take 20 seconds a day to ask your daily Magic Question, you are getting your brain's full attention. If you ask this question out loud, you might even get your brain's attention even faster.

Your brain might ignore affirming sticky notes spread around your house, but it cannot ignore a new auditory transmission coming from your mouth. That is the power of asking these questions out loud, at least once a day.

I could spend another 100 pages showing you diagrams of the brain, and using medical words that would make your eyes glaze over. However, I have includes some footnotes to some articles if you are interested in reading the medical research. For me, I just like to know this is not some whacky new technique that only works because I believe it works.

No, I don't believe this technique is psychosomatic in any way. I think it is simply a powerful trick to get your mind scanning the world, and noticing and creating opportunities that your brain might have been missing up until now.

The diagram below shows you a bit about how information comes into your brain from the five senses. The common attitude is that the RAS is not a specific cluster of nerve cells in the brain that you can touch. Scientists refer to it more as a system, like an overriding computer operation system using the various parts of the brain to execute its commands.

The Reticular Activating System

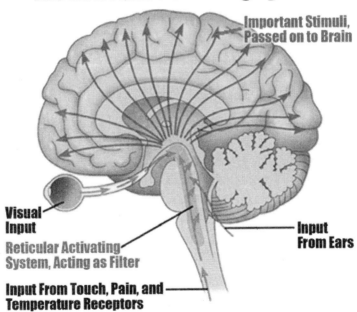

Important Stimuli, Passed on to Brain

Visual Input

Reticular Activating System, Acting as Filter

Input From Touch, Pain, and Temperature Receptors

Input From Ears

The Jimmy Metaphor

Jimmy, the Most Annoying Person on Earth

This concept of directing your mind is often misunderstood or difficult to make clear and easy. So, after many years of explaining it the long way, I came up with the perfect metaphor.

Before I share the metaphor, I feel compelled to thank my grumpy neighbor for illustrating it so perfectly. I remember moving into a new place in Sherman Oaks, CA, and taking 10 minutes to be kind to one of my neighbors. My friend, Mel, was at my house, helping me unpack. This 62-year-old, long-haired hippie said "hello". We will call him 'Jimmy'.

I offered Jimmy a glass of wine and thought it would be nice to take a short break from unpacking. Almost 90 minutes later, neither Mel nor I had said three full sentences. But, to our enlightenment, we now knew every problem in the neighborhood, every person who'd lied to Jimmy, cheated him, and even the truth about the death of Janis Joplin. Wow, we were exhausted. When I finally convinced him to leave, we were stunned. The combination of anger, talkativeness, and pessimism was so overwhelming... we needed more wine! Jimmy had a unique ability to find everything wrong with the world and fixate his entire being on complaining about it.

Over the next few months, every single time I ran into Jimmy, he would skip the formalities of saying hello and just start to rant about his landlord, the roofers, the government, and anything else he was pissed off about at that moment. He was like a bulldog. If there was anything on the planet to complain about, he felt it was his job to put a spotlight on it and tell anyone within earshot.

Finally, I asked him politely to please stop complaining around me. I explained that I don't watch the local news because it is all bad news of murders and criminal activity. I don't complain or blame people, because it serves no useful purpose. My dad used to tell me this hysterical quote, "Don't tell people your problems. Half of them don't care and the other half are glad it happened to you."

Jimmy was a bit confused. He said, "I don't complain a lot. I'm just telling you what's going on. I replied, "No, you are telling me what is going on in your mind, with your filters, your beliefs, and solely focusing on your problems, not solutions. Just to be clear, if you can't speak to me without complaining, accusing, or cussing, please don't talk to me at all."

I haven't spoken to Jimmy since then.

Jimmy gave me a gift. With his incredibly polished mental skills that were 60-years'-hardwired into his brain, he scanned the world for problems and found them. He went to bed scanning the world for problems and woke up wanting to find more problems. The more problems he found, the better he felt about his own failed life. The more bad people he could blame, the better he felt about the fact that he rode a bicycle around town because he couldn't afford a car. Each time his rent was due was a great excuse to complain about the prices and the economy, and it made him feel better about not having a job for 10 years, etc.

Jimmy's brain was a highly-tuned Problem Radar. Jimmy saw problems where none existed and blew them out of proportion. His brain and mouth were "complaint machines".

Mel and I dubbed him the "Most Annoying Person on Earth". However, in truth, Jimmy simply had no control over his thoughts. He had no awareness of the R.A.S inside his mind. And, he was the unhappiest human being I've ever met. I have compassion, but have no desire to get close enough to help. He is like a toxic cloud of negativity; if you get in close, he will rain on you.

Jimmy had a specific mental process for making himself totally unhappy. He was probably not aware of it, but studying the polar opposite of what you want to become is useful. By figuring out which way is North, you can easily travel South.

Jimmy did one thing better than most of us. He asked himself internal questions like, "Who is to blame?, What's wrong today?, What can I find to complain about today?, Who is going to try to cheat me today?, etc." Then, his brain efficiently and effectively scanned his world to find answers.

My brain, your brain, and Jimmy's brain are all excellent scanners of information. The only difference is in the instructions you, Jimmy, and I put into our brains.

Quality Questions Can Dislodge Even The Most Stubborn Mental Habits

If you grew up in a poor family or had a "scarcity mentality" for whatever reason, you probably have some beliefs that indicate there is a lack of money in the world. If you grew up around people who stole things, or wore used clothes and hand-me-down shoes, then you might have adopted the belief that expensive things are hard to get if you are honest. These limiting beliefs, although not conscious, do drive your behavior. Asking a different set of questions can dislodge these old beliefs.

When an opportunity falls into a person's lap, some people look for the reasons it will not work. Before reading this book you might have said, "This is too easy. This is too good to be true. Money doesn't grow on trees. How could an opportunity come along that easily? What is the catch?"

These poorly-chosen questions cripple your chances of success and stop you from taking action.

The last question sabotages what could be a good thing. If you ask any question enough times, your mind will find an answer. This truth can work for you or against you.

So, your brain finds some catch, and you miss an opportunity to cash in on some good luck.

You must learn to scratch out the limiting beliefs and reprogram a solution-based frame of the world. Even if you have a bucket full of real-life bad experiences, parents with crappy attitudes, and $60,000 in credit card debt, you can leapfrog past your limiting beliefs using empowering questions.

Affirmations are deceiving. You might say to yourself, "I am skinny. I am good-looking. I am rich." And your mind is thinking, "No, you're not." Right?

Affirmations aren't congruent. Affirmations have sort of a mixed result. Some people say they work, but some people say they don't because you really need to change the belief systems at your core, and then also understand that you need to take gradual steps, so that you can begin to notice things.

The easiest way to change belief systems is to ask better questions, and the results will erode old beliefs.

Beliefs show up in a person's words and actions. However, the power of internal dialogue (self-talk) and the words you use are full of the belief systems you hold as true. Changing your internal belief system is a conversation too large for this short book. The secret to changing those belief systems lies in the structure of beliefs, your experiences, and even the pre-suppositions and frames with which you view the world. The easiest way to change that frame and make a new pre-supposition is by asking well-crafted Magic Questions. Seriously, it's much easier and cheaper than years of coach therapy. The last section of this book explains in perfect detail the sentence structure for building the perfect belief-busting Magic Question.

8 The Happiness Radar

Here is the perfect metaphor for this phenomenon:
The Happiness Radar.

Imagine your brain as a control tower on a battleship in the middle of the ocean. Instead of one radar system, you have dozens. You have the happiness radar, the misery radar, the problem radar, the failure radar, the beauty radar, the peace radar, the self-critical radar, the 'I hate the president radar', the 'the world is going to end radar', etc.

You can choose which radar you want to turn on and which ones you want to turn off.

The happiness radar is simple to activate. Just write the following words on an index card and read it a few times a day:

"What is another reason to be happy now?"

While this sentence seems simple, it is linguistically elegant because it pre-supposed that there was already another reason to be happy. (Now your brain is finding two things, not just one.) And, it has an embedded command to be happy right now; now... not in the future. You could create a slight variation of this sentence like this...

"How many things can I find to be happy about now?"

"How many reasons can I discover to be incredibly happy?"

"Scan the world for reasons to be happy."

"Show me the many reasons that it's okay to be joyous right now."

Asking the question is part one. Finding the answers it part two. You must allocate 60 seconds a day to answer this question 5-12 times a day, every day. This mental process must become a habit. You will be re-wiring your brain and creating new, stronger, neural pathways each time to answer these questions.

Do this every day for 21 days... you will be happier.

It's like a Thermostat inside your Brain.

Whatever your life looks like today is due to your thermostat being set there.

So what we have to do is change the thermostat. You have to actually program a new thermostat at a different vibrational frequency, so that currently you are hot! Oh my God, I'm so hot! I have to take some action to get cool! You're going to be so uncomfortable in the current situation, you'll take action. If you're too comfortable, you get lazy.

Author John Assaraf used this metaphor of a thermostat, which is very interesting.

He says, "For example, any liquid-cooled car engine has a small device called the **thermostat** that sits between the engine and the radiator. The thermostat in most cars is about two inches (five cm) in diameter. Its job is to block the flow of coolant to the radiator until the engine has warmed up. When the engine is cold, no coolant flows through the engine. Once the engine reaches its set temperature (generally about 200 degrees F, 95 degrees C), the thermostat opens. By letting the engine warm up as quickly as possible, the thermostat reduces engine wear, deposits, and emissions. It's really amazing and, if you could see how does its work, it's like magic!"

Now, I don't want to force you to be uncomfortable, but I'm suggesting that if you take small steps to change your comfort level, so that you're not fully comfortable, it'll motivate you to make some changes...because you've got to take a few more actions.

I didn't have to get up and go the gym this morning, I could have slept another 30, 40 minutes, but it's important to me to be fit. In fact, I'm uncomfortable when I look fat.

I know a woman who is beautiful and thin, and she perceives herself as fat when the whole world sees her as thin.

Literally, two pounds makes her really uncomfortable, eight pounds makes her sick. Eight pounds is like no, no, no, not eating that! Nope!

She is motivated out of her own uncomfortable-ness. She gets highly uncomfortable about four pounds of weight.

I see people who weigh 400 pounds. In their case, four pounds are irrelevant. They can't be comfortable at that weight. But, this woman's four pounds makes her so uncomfortable, she takes massive action.

So the question is: how do you change it? You change it through habitual thinking processes. You change it through changing your internal dialogue. You change it through habits. You change it through increasing your ability to confront reality.

The magic question has been the single-most effective technique for changing the direction of my thoughts and attracting prosperity that I've ever discovered. If you look in the mirror and don't like what you see... change your questions first and quiet any negative voices which contain judgment. Tell them to shut up, and turn all your internal voices into question generators.

What can I eat today that is nutritious? How much fun will it be to exercise today? How hot will I look when I get firm and ripped?

9 How I Use the Magic Questions

The Power of the Index Card

You see, I've been using the Magic Question technique for years. It wasn't until recently that I recognized the physical system which I was using that inspired me to write this short book.

- The fact that I turned my goals and desires into questions was a profound shift and deviation from what most other goal-setting books are teaching.

- The fact that I take those questions and physically write them with a bold black sharpie marker on a brightly-colored index card is unique. I also think writing them in my own handwriting personalizes them to me. My unconscious likes that.

- The fact that I put these small, colorful index cards around my house and office is unique. When I go to bed, there is one card on my bedside table. That forces me to read that question and contemplate the answer while I sleep. When I get out of the shower, there is a neon-green index card on my mirror, giving me food for thought when I brush my teeth and dry my hair. When I go to the coffeemaker each morning, there is a bright-orange index card with yet another magic question begging to be answered.

No matter what my little hamster-wheel monkey-mind was thinking when I walked into that room, I notice the index card, stop, read it, and become consciously aware that the question needs answers.

As soon as they figure out how to make waterproof index cards, you can bet one will be in the shower. Everyone gets their best ideas in the shower.

I ask questions like, "How can I get healthier and have more energy?" Then, my brain reminds me of things like the $300 juicer in my cabinet, the vitamins I bought last month, and the gym membership which I haven't used in two weeks. My brain finds answers to solve specific useful problems.

You might have asked, "How can I be happier and more successful?"

The result is that you've invested time into reading this book. This is just one of many options your brain will continue to provide... if you keep asking the right questions.

I actually write one question a day on an index card, and leave them around the house to surprise myself on a daily basis. I find it. I read it out loud. Then, my mental wheels start turning.

POWERFUL SELF-TALK

I have found that when you ask questions to yourself, your unconscious mind gives you answers.

By doing this, you have to consciously ask yourself well-composed questions.

According to University of Queensland, with its study of how senses influence the sum of our experiences, the consistent feeding of the conscious mind affects the subconscious mind.

Where is the red in this room? Where is the green in this room? You found it, right? Where's the gold? You found it!

So even if you don't know the answer, if you ask the question every day, your brain begins working on that. And one of the easy techniques, especially when you have a problem, let's say you have a spousal problem or you don't know if you should quit your job, you don't know how to handle a conflict, if you simply release it to the universe, ask the question, "How do I improve my marriage?"

Take that question, and write it down where you will see it a few times a day. I've seen people put in on their screensaver on their computer, on a post-it note on the dashboard of their car, or on a piece of paper next to the toothpaste. The trick to place it somewhere you'll see the question every day. You don't have to work on the question or the solution. Just see it. Read it. Let it sit in your mind and percolate.

So here're some examples, "How can I pay off my debt quickly? How can I double my income? What's the fastest way I can attract $5000 dollars?"

Do you see how these questions are useful, and direct your mind in finding multiple answers?

They are well-crafted, linguistically-clever questions which pre-suppose that an answer is possible, and allow your brain to work on finding answers

In my life, I simply pick one question on an index card, and I place it on my bathroom mirror. So, I read it at least twice a day.

Don't put 20 questions on 20 index cards on your bathroom sink; you'll overwhelm yourself. What happens if you have 20 stickers and notecards? Your brain will begin to simply not see them anymore. You will stop reading them because your brain has a hard time handling 20 different bits of information at the exact same time. Just choose one question a day, and keep that question active until your brain has had time to come up with some creative solutions. I've seen people use the same question for one day, one month, even one year.

You can put one question in the kitchen and one at your office desk. I'm suggesting that you just don't overdo it.

Here are some more questions which you might find useful... "How can I make a million dollars? How can I experience more freedom while earning money?"

Notice that these questions are very well-phrased. The structure of the question is the key.

The Structure of a Well-Crafted, Question

Don't create a question which results in internal criticism.
Avoid questions like, "How come I'm fat?"

If I say "How come I'm fat", what answers will I get? My
brain will give me many reasons why I'm fat. What's worse,
the reasons I get from the sentence structure pre-suppose and
confirm the belief that I am fat. Not empowering.

So why don't you ask, "Why am I broke?"

Your inner voice might respond with comments like "Because
you're lazy or Because you're untalented." These are answers
which are not empowering. Inner talk like this leads to
depression and hesitation. In many cases, it begins to erode a
person's self-esteem. None of this is helping you find solutions
to your financial problems. The focus becomes the problems,
not the solutions. The key to a good question is wording it in a
specific language structure which creates a "solution frame".

Again, don't ask a question which results in negative answers.
There is a time and place for looking at your life through a
lens of authenticity and brutal honesty. Evaluating any bad
habits and working to change them can be useful. The Magic
Question technique is not that time. If you drink too much
or don't exercise, you probably already are aware of these
non-optimal habits. Instead of dwelling on these short-
term bad habits, you can reframe these issues into Magic
Questions while focusing on solutions, not rehashing the
problem.

The goal of this chapter is to easily recognize a well-crafted Magic Question, which only has good answers or great answers that empower you.

So what I'd like you to do is read the list of questions below and decide whether or not they are effective and useful questions.

Why do I keep spending all my money?

Why do I have no self-control?

Why can't I get a raise?

Are these good questions? Yes? No?

Those are terrible questions! In fact, you will notice all of the above questions start with 'why'. In general, I avoid questions with 'why' and you should, too. While there might be a question that contains the word 'why', which *will* be empowering, in general you could replace the 'why' with 'how' and create an even better question.

For example, you could write down "Why am I so awesome?" This is not a bad question. It pre-supposes that you are awesome. Your brain looks in the now and in the past to find reasons why you are, indeed, so awesome. However, part of the inherent brilliance of a well-crafted Magic Question is for your brain to look in the now and the future. The future is where you can make changes and improve. I would coach this person to change the question to "What can I do today to be even more awesome?"

Granted, this is a silly question, which you might not find yourself using. But it illustrates the point quite well. As a general rule, avoid 'why' questions.

So let's identify some "good" and "bad" questions.

Why am I always failing? *Bad*

Why can't I get a raise? *Bad*

Why am I not taller? *Bad*

Why am I so fat? *Bad*

How can I easily pay off this debt? *Good*

How sexy do I look today? *Good*

How sexy is my husband? *Good*

How much fun are we having? *Good*

Why can't I ever get ahead in life? *Bad*

Why is my relationship so miserable? *Bad*

Why don't I have enough money? *Bad*

How can I find enough money? *Good*

How much fun will it be to be rich? *Good*

Now you get it. Do you see the difference?

What steps do I need to take to start my own business now? *Good*

How easy would it be to get a $10,000 raise in my income this year? *Good*

What are my best options for earning extra money? *Good*

Now, write some questions on a piece of paper and evaluate the quality of the questions. What area of your life did you decide to work on; money, career, love?

Ask a question related to your relationship. Write it down. Make it empowering. If you find a great question, make two or three variations on that same question.

Here are some examples:

- How do I get my ideas heard and adhered to?

- What can I do to transform the lives of my loved ones, and help them to grow and progress as individuals?

- How can I get more money by working less?

- How can I enrich the lives of others, while enriching my life at the same time?

- How can I excel in my career, and have the time, freedom, money and opportunities to see the world?

- How can I get to be the healthiest and fittest that I have ever been?

So, basically it's just "How can I be the healthiest, how can I be the happiest, how can I have the most energy, what foods can I eat?"

- How can I be a money-magnet?

- What are the great opportunities and investments for me now?

Nice. What are the great opportunities? Or what investments or great opportunities, either way you want to do that. Okay? So here is what I would do to wrap up this section to make it incredibly useful for you

10 Wealth and Goal Setting

Knowledge without Action is Dead

Our minds are excuse-making machines. They release what they are fed. Now, you have to choose questions wisely, and determine whether it is beneficial to your welfare or do what pleases you. You are the one who will reap the fruits anyway. SOOOOO, my advice is that you take control of it or else it will control you.

The neat thing about this exercise is that it is not a goal exercise. The application is a neuro-training exercise to create new neuropathways to find things you didn't see before.

If I input a goal and then a target, then that's goal-setting which can be useful.

This is really designed to exercise the synaptic pathways in your brain to begin to see colors and things you wouldn't normally see.

John Vokey said in an interview for an online course at University of Queensland, "Colors are something we bring to our interpretation of things, but it's not to say that it's an accurate reflection of reality. Why I say that is because, evolutionarily speaking, we look at things like berries-they go out of their way to make themselves a bright red to contrast with the green so you'll eat them – so it's to some sense in the world, too, but it's more of an act that you bring to the world. I think that's true for most of the world. I think that's true for most perception. It's a mistake to put it in the world, as much as we all agree on it. Remember, the important thing is that you get through the world without falling into holes, bumping into things, or getting eaten by lions, but that's it. What you perceive, what you construct to perceive, just has to meet those criteria. It doesn't really matter that it actually matches the world in any other sense. It just has to match the world so you can maneuver your way through it, which might be a good argument. There's a good chance that maybe the way you perceive the world is nothing like how your dog does. There are people out there who want to make better decisions, think better and do better."

When you ask the right questions, your brain will find solutions. Now, you might go and ask, "What's the fastest way I can earn $5,000?" Your first answer might be "sell myself into slavery" and you're like, that's a horrible and terrible idea. For me, I don't think I'd get $5000, frankly.

You agree? Think... think...umm... I could rob a bank. Terrible idea. But here's what I do...you can judge the idea as you want but it's like brainstorming. Have you ever done brainstorming? The idea of brainstorming is not to be too judgmental.

So, you ask the question enough that it will allow you to go deeper. Resilience in doing this process is magical!

So remember the good in this new mind-game, it's easy the first couple of days, it's easy. But then you gotta go deeper. By doing this repetition, it plays a vital role in the entire progression. You'll find yourself being bored, you may come up with all the answers and you'll sit and say "ok, this doesn't work. I've come up with 20 different ways to earn $5000 quickly." But if you keep asking the questions, you're tuning into something you didn't know before.

People do this exercise and they get phone calls out of the blue, they remember they met somebody five years ago, they see somebody on Facebook or LinkedIn and are like "Wow! Now that I'm looking for it, that guy does refinancing! Maybe Jim knows how to do it or somebody who does." And if you are beholden to it, then you start asking different questions like "Jim, I know you don't do this, but I'm trying to find $5,000 for this project I'm working on. Who do you know?" And you would never have asked that question before if you didn't ask the question in your brain that enlightened you enough to see the opportunity.

"Who will I meet who will be the key to doubling my income?" Great question, because now you're scanning the world looking for who you're going to meet.

"Where can I find a new job that pays me what I'm worth?" I assume that's a good question if you have good self-worth. If you have bad self-worth, wait a while on that one.

"How, specifically, can I make a million dollars? Or 10 million Blat or 10 million Rupees?"

"How, specifically, can I experience more freedom while earning more money?" That's a great question, because lots of people associate making lots of money with losing their time.

"I'm going to make lots of money, but then I'm going to have responsibility and now, if I need to be committed, I can't be a good parent to my kids and then they're going to be unhappy, so I can't make too much money because that means I don't have enough time." You know this is in your brain. It's a worldwide, viral, self-sabotaging thought. It's a trait that people think it's a trade-off.

There is a way to do it. Time management. Do your research; you will be surprised how many tens of thousands of people are already doing this. As you go on you will innovate a unique combination of who you are with what you supplement in your mind.

How to Build a Business with Both Revenue and Freedom

I interviewed Sam Carpenter, the author of the book *Work the System*. His story is remarkable because he almost lost his marriage and health due to working 80 hours a week for 16 years straight, running his company. Because he asked the right question and found a solution to that question, he figured out a way to work just two hours and have more profit.

Actually, his company brings in twice as much money as it did before. He spends a lot of time with his family, and he has his health back. How did he do that? I will encourage you to read his book to discover his answers. The important point here is that, for 16 years, he was asking the wrong questions.

After years of putting out fires and being the problem-solver at all levels of his growing telephone answering service, he was emotionally spent. He finally asked this question:

"Is there a system that can help me run my business well when I'm not there?"

It turned out that there wasn't such a system which was perfect for his exact business, so he created one. It wasn't simple, but within about a year, he was free and his business was booming. I imagine that his Magic Question was a series of smaller questions and was probably refined over the year. Based on his desire to have the highest quality customer service and provide happy long-term employees, I imagine his final Magic Question read something like this:

"What management system can I create that motivates and empowers my employees to handle all the day-to-day operations with amazing quality, efficiency, and profit... without me being there?"

Now, I didn't ask Sam if he wrote this question out on an index card and read it every day. But, I do know he was asking some version of that question day in and day out because of his relentless actions which resulted in a company-wide makeover, from writing a procedure to replacing the toilet paper roll, depositing checks in the bank, and hiring only employees who passed a drug test.

Tim Ferris wrote a best-selling book called *The Four Hour Workweek,* which was the result of Tim asking himself the question, "How can I build a business that allows me to work just four hours a week from anywhere in the world?" Tim gives you his answers in his book. Neither one of these men would have developed an entirely new business paradigm without first asking a question, which demanded freedom for themselves as part of the answer.

Years ago, I began asking myself this question, ""What business projects can I invest time into today that will make money while I sleep the rest of my life?"

For me, the answer was to write books and create information products which continue to provide royalties and residual income 20+ years after they were created.

What if I was 22 years old and asked this short-sighted question, "What can I do that makes me the most money per hour this year?" In all probability, I would have found a high-paying hourly wage job. That might have been useful for then, but it would have provided no residual income years later.

My questions change year to year. If I'm feeling too burdened by management tasks, I spend a month asking a question like this:

"What has to happen in order for me to own an international publishing company which does not require me to manage it on a day-to-day basis?"

That is a better question, which provides a bigger, more satisfying answer. Naturally, this question, "How can I get a better paying job?" is better than this question, "Why can't I find a better paying job." The last question is horrible. Remember, as a general rule, I avoid 'why' questions.

Still, today, I find myself asking questions relating to residual income.

- How can I create products that bring in residual income?

- What job can I do to create residual income?

- What investments can I make that are low-risk and high-return?

I have developed key questions to help evaluate business opportunities. Now that I am a well-known international speaker, I get proposals all the time from some incredibly smart and successful people.

My heart tells me to say yes to all of them. But, my logic and criteria allow me to sort and reject, based on my values. The idea of values is discussed in detail in my book, *The Success Secrets of the Rich and Happy*. I think the exercise is profound for those readers who have not ever gone through the process of listing their top three values relating to career, relationships, health, etc.

For me, I always want to have the emotion of making a difference, creativity, fun, and profit in most of the new projects I take on. I also pay special attention to the emotion of freedom and variety. This keeps me from getting bored and feeling trapped in any one job or project.

Knowing my personal value helps me create better questions, which helps me to better sort out the business opportunities so that I can see clearly if they are congruent with my life's mission, or if they're only a distraction.

It sorts what projects I say "yes" to and helps me feel good about saying "no" to other projects.

If you come to me and say, "Bart, I want to be your business partner. We are going to make $10 million. All that is required of you, Bart, is to be on the phone eight hours a day, seven days a week from our corporate office in Des Moines, Iowa."

I would probably kindly say, "That doesn't match my model of my ideal career. I'm going to have to pass on that proposal."

If I did say yes to that business opportunity, I'd be giving up my freedom, giving up my creative projects, and not building anything with residual income. I know I need to sort for opportunities that match my values.

My values might be very different from your values.

I started writing books over 20 years ago. I really started asking the question, "What projects can I start today that will make me residual income for the rest of my life?"

Because that was a reoccurring question, I created a library of audio products, videos, seminars, and numerous books.

Don't get me wrong; it doesn't mean it's always easy. It doesn't mean everything works. I failed a lot. I still fail a lot. Most of the answers to the Magic Question are not the best answers. That is why I asked it repeatedly and carefully evaluate or test the answers I get.

My Magic Question is like creating a daily brainstorming session in my own brain. All answers are accepted and not judged at the time. Then, later, I evaluate them all and reject the ones which seem to not fit me. Without enough creative thinking and time to process it, I usually find one or two great answers to my Magic Question.

Meditation and Incantation

Meditation can be very useful. You can even meditate on a Magic Question. By helping you let go of the distractions that have been clouding your mind, meditation will sharpen your focus to levels you didn't think possible. I know this from my personal experience. Meditation has been scientifically proven to reduce stress, bad cholesterol, and a whole host of other maladies. The biggest benefit might just be increased self-awareness, and even enlightenment. I'm suggesting you leverage this powerful, age-tested technique to throw in a few questions during your next meditation

When you sit quietly and let your mind settle, all the innovative, inventive, and inspired ideas that have been hiding out in the depths of your mind are going to begin to bubble to the surface. The connection between stillness and creativity is powerful. I suggest simply holding a single question in your mind's awareness and ask it about every two minutes during your meditation.

The Linguistic Structure

Now, this is perhaps the most important chapter in the book. The structure of the question and what words you use and don't use are incredibly important. If you use a poorly-structured sentence, you send your brain looking for the wrong information.

For example, if you give a bicycle messenger the wrong address to go pick up an important packet of documents, it is unlikely he will return with the packet. The key is giving the correct INPUT so you get the best OUTPUT.

The structure of language can be very complicated, but powerful. The famous psychiatrist, Milton Erickson, was a pioneer in using tricky, powerful sentence structure to change life-long habits, heal the sick, remove traumas, and generally transform his patients with nothing more than his words. If you are not familiar with the pioneering work of Milton Erickson, let me give you some context as to his situation. Near the end of his life, he was limited in both mobility and movement. His voice was timid and at times difficult to understand. Because he was limited to a wheelchair and physically had limited movement, his voice was his only tool. However, not just his voice, but his choice of words was arguably the most flexible tool at this disposal to elicit change and communicate with his patients. No deep, resounding, powerful tone shifts. No body language to create a sense of power or even respect. He was a frail man trapped in a failing body, with his words as his tool for change. Perhaps because of these limitations, he crafted an entire breakthrough sequence of words that changed beliefs in a short period of time. In fact, listening to recordings of Erickson, it is difficult to even stay awake and attempt to unwrap the layers of sentences which often seem random to the casual listener. In a word...genius.

If the structure of language really interests you, I recommend you read the book, Sleight of Mouth, by Robert Diltz.

I'm not even going to attempt to unwrap and decipher the dozens of linguistic patterns in the book. I'm only going to extrapolate and explain the one powerful aspect of the questions, which I believe was one cornerstone of how he successfully elicited instant and lasting change in his patients.

Principle #1: Embed positive pre-suppositions.

The word 'pre-supposition' comes from the word presuppose, or 'before the idea in question'. The most common and amusing example of this is the famous comic question, "When did you stop beating your wife?"

If you answer with a time or date, you've lost in both cases. The instinctive answer is to come up with a date. But, the question pre-supposes that you did beat your wife. It's a loaded question, which can't be answered without incriminating yourself.

Another example comes from politics down under, "Should

a smack as part of good parental correction be a criminal offence in New Zealand?"

Murray Edridge, of Barnardos, New Zealand, criticized the question as "loaded and ambiguous" and claimed "the question presupposes that smacking is a part of good parental correction". She was correct; the question was a loaded question, embedded with the presupposition.

This same type of linguistic trickery can be used for good, on your own brain.

Here is an example of a 50-year-old female seminar participant struggling with body-image issues. After analyzing her handwriting, we both agreed that her self-image was lower than was either deserved or desired. I asked her to give me an example of the internal voice in her head that caused her to feel badly about her body. She said, "When I look in the mirror and see my body, I have a voice that criticizes what I see and notices all the flaws." She had the awareness that the internal voice was both partly a function of her inner child not feeling good enough, and partly because she didn't have the athletic body of her youth. So, instead of arguing with her internal voice and debating the visual facts, we proposed a Magic Question, which changed her life every morning in front of the mirror. I had her write two questions to choose from.

1. How hot do I look today?

2. What part of my body looks sexy today?

She chose both questions and decided to ask them every day, regardless of the other, less-useful, critical voice. She asked me why these questions instantly made her feel better the minute she asked them.

The answer was embedded in the question. In order to answer the question, her mind had to assume that she *did* look hot today, and at least some parts of her body looked sexy. Now, her brain went to work finding aspects of her body that did look sexy and did look hot.

So, lesson one...make sure your question pre-supposes that the answer exists, and that the answer is based on something positive. Even without a profound presupposition, the mere fact that you are asking the question pre-supposes that an answer exists.

Principle #2: Avoid the Negative

Do not frame the question in a negative sense.

Using words like NOT, CAN'T, WON'T, and DON'T usually elicits reasons why you do NOT have something, as opposed to finding solutions as to how you can get something. For example, the following are terrible questions, which only create more reasons to get depressed:

Why can't I ever get a break? Why won't anything good ever happen to me? Why don't I have any money? Why don't women find me attractive?

The only answers you would get from those crappy questions are answers that CONFIRM your worst fears and doubts. Don't do that.

Principle #3: Frame the question to look for answers from the present or future

This is essential, because you want to move toward what you want, not look back at what you did wrong in the past. The question of "Why am I such a failure?" only brings up past events or past emotions, which confirm the un-empowering pre-supposition that you are a failure. While not a good question, "How can I avoid failing in the future?" would be better than the first question, but still crappy. Why? You have to visualize what you don't want (failure) in order to make sense of the question at all. You only want images in your head that elicit positive emotions. If failure is an issue for you, take the opposite of failure, which is success, and build a question for what you are moving toward, not away from. "How can I be even more successful this month?" This pre-supposes that you are successful already. This looks forward into the future. And there is nothing negative in the sentence.

Principle #4: Avoid the Word 'Why'

The final general rule is to avoid the word 'Why' in your magic question sentence structure. There are exceptions to this, but 'Why' sentences are fraught with the tendency to turn negative, not positive.

Remember, you can think of the outcome as a puzzle which needs to be solved; the puzzle of how to be more fit, happier, richer, or get a new car. A puzzle has lots of answers and puzzles rarely have an A or B answer.

The Basic Magic Question Sentence Structure

So, in the beginning of this fun and playful mental conditioning ritual, you will want to use the basic CORE sentence structure as follows:

QUESTION WORD + PUZZLE

In English grammar, the common question words are as follows:

WHO

WHO is only used when referring to people (I want to know the person).

- Who do I know who can help me with this decision?

- Who among my close friends will join me in this adventure?

- Who has friends who need to hear about this opportunity?

WHERE

WHERE is used when referring to a place or location (I want to know the place).

- Where can I find more people who need this opportunity?

- Where would provide my family with an amazing vacation?

- Where are the intelligent people in this town?

WHEN

WHEN is used to refer to a time or an occasion
(I want to know the time).

- When can I expect a miracle?

- When is the best time to tell her the good news?

- When will a person show up in my life to love?

WHAT

WHAT is used to refer to specific information
(I want to know the thing).

- What application can I create to change the world?

- What value can I create to serve my customers better?

- What would be the most creative expression of my soul?

WHICH

WHICH is used to make a choice
(I want to know the alternatives).

- Which investment has the most profit with the least risk?

- Which day will the good news come?

- Which house will provide the best home for my family?

HOW

HOW is used to describe the manner in which something is done (I want to know the way).

- How many ways can I think of to be romantic?

- How do I always come up with the right decision?

- How can I learn Spanish quickly, and with adventure?

With **HOW**, there are a number of other expressions that are used in questions:

How much refers to a quantity or a price (uncountable nouns).

- How much fun can I have while recovering from this disease?

- How much money can I make this month?

- How much money can I raise for my new business?

How many refers to a quantity (countable nouns).

- How many days will be filled with fascination and love this month?

- How many people can I attract to my social media tribe?

- How many ways can I think of to reward my employees?

How often refers to frequency.

- How often do you visit your grandmother?

- How can I find business partners this month?

- How often can I find reasons to be happy today?

How far refers to distance.

- How far can I get in this new career?

- How far can I run in this next exercise?

PUZZLE is my word for the CHALLENGE or PROBLEM you want to solve.

I prefer the word 'Puzzle', because puzzles are fun and can be solved.

So, after your Question Word, you would add the Puzzle: "Make a million dollars", "Find a better job", "Make my wife feel loved", "Get money for college".

These two key pieces are enough to have an effective Magic Question. Naturally, you will want to add a pronoun, such as I, he, she, them, etc.

Simple Structure

QUESTION WORD + PROUNOUN + PUZZLE

Example:

How can I get money for college? Who will I meet who will bring me true love? How can my business double its revenue this quarter?

Advanced Structure

SOFTENER + MAGIC WORD + QUESTION WORD + PROUNOUN + PUZZLE

Softener:

A softener is a phrase that helps lower unconscious resistance to an upcoming command or comment. It softens the jolt of the upcoming sentence.

A magic word is one in a series of hypnotic words that enhances the emotional state of the listener and increases the persuasive power of the words coming after it.

For example, to increase the fun and effectiveness of any Magic Question, you could turn a Simple Structure Question into an Advanced Structure Question like this:

Simple:

How can I get plenty of money for college?

Advanced:

I'm beginning to wonder **how** *effortlessly* **I can get money for college.**

Softener: *I'm beginning to wonder*

Magic word: *effortlessly*

Not only is this linguistically-hypnotic in nature, but it is more fun to say.

Here are my favorite Magic Words to use in the questions.

Naturally
Effortlessly
Automatically

Here are my favorite Softeners to use in these questions:

When I...
If I were to...
What's it like when I...
A person can...
What if I could...
I'm wondering...

Here are some of my favorite verbs for these questions. Verbs appear in the Puzzle portion of the formula.

Get	Envision
Attract	Manifest
Earn	Begin
Become	Expand
Create	Discover
Experience	

NOW YOU PUT THEM ALL TOGETHER.

QUESTION WORD + PROUNOUN + PUZZLE

The first step is to write down the PUZZLE.

Think about the problem you want to solve, and turn it into a puzzle with unlimited answers.

Puzzle: _____

> *Get more money*

Then, add the Question Word

> *How*

Then add the Pronoun

> *I*

Put them all together

"How do I get more money?"

Then, if you are feeling fancy, add a softener or magic word to make the sentence more interesting.

"I'm wondering how easily it could be to get more money."

or

"I'm wondering what fun opportunities I can discover to get more money."

The next section has pre-written, off-the-shelf Magic Questions.

12   Glossary of Magic Questions

Money

- ? How can I double my income?

- ? How can I attract a better job?

- ? How can I make more money per month?

- ? How can I work smarter?

- ? How can I work less for more money?

- ? How quickly can I pay off this debt?

- ? How can I increase my income now?

- ? What is the fastest way I can earn $5000?

- ? What's the fastest way I can earn 500,000 rupees?

- ? What's the fastest way I can earn five million Euros?"

Career

- ? What's the best career for me?

- ? I'm beginning to wonder what's the best career for me where I can make plenty of money and have plenty of time with my family?

? What motivates me to build a better career?

? How much fun is it to build my career?

? How can I easily attract a supportive team around me?

? How can I inspire and lead my team?

? Who do I know who needs an opportunity like this?

? Who is the most successful person I know?

? How can I get referrals from friends to get involved in this project?

? Who will I meet today who needs my help?

? Who will I magically meet today who will be open to this business opportunity?

? How much fun will it be to have a team of 20 successful distributors?

? What ways can I discover to double my sales?

? Who do I know that can help fund my new business?

? Who do I know who could help me find a better job?

? Who do I know that can invest in this start-up?

? Who do I know that knows someone that does venture capital to launch this start-up wildly successfully?

? Who do I know who could help me solve this problem?

? What else can I do to earn extra money this month?

Relationships

? What's a clever way to make my spouse feel loved?

? How much fun is it to be in a loving relationship?

? I wonder how soon I will meet my next lover?

? How great is my connection with my spouse?

? What are the many reasons I love _____?

? How many wonderful qualities does _____ bring to my life?

? How many wonderful qualities does _____ uniquely possess?

Health

? How can I easily lose weight safely?

? How much fun will it be to work out today?

? How quickly can my healthy body be evident in the mirror?

? Who can I talk to about being a workout buddy and help to keep me accountable in my goals?

? What foods that taste good have no sugar?

② What foods that taste good have no gluten?

② How can I easily eat five small, protein-packed meals a day?

② What options do I have for eating nutritiously during a busy day?

② How easily will it be to choose nutritious foods today?

② How great does it feel after I work out?

② How great mentally do I feel after I work out?

② What foods do I need to look for and buy at the grocery store to make me feel better and healthy?

② How can I keep my body in alkaline balance without sacrificing tasty food?

② What can I eat for breakfast that gives me energy and keeps me fit?

② Where can I find healthy, fit people to spend time with?

② What can I do on a Friday night that increases my health and fills me with joy?

② How hot do I look today?

② How sexy does my body look today?

② What parts of my body look fit today?

Spirituality

⟨?⟩ How good do I feel when I meditate?

⟨?⟩ How close can I feel to my God today?

⟨?⟩ How much wiser do I feel when I am in touch with my inner spirit?

⟨?⟩ What lessons are there to be learned today?

⟨?⟩ How can I be in touch with my higher self easily?

⟨?⟩ Who has the same beliefs as I and can share my spiritual journey with me?

⟨?⟩ Who can I meet who enhances my spiritual life?

⟨?⟩ What groups of like-minded spiritual people can I join?

⟨?⟩ Where can I find more like-minded activity partners?

Travel

⟨?⟩ How much adventure am I going to have when I get to Thailand?

⟨?⟩ How easy can I be to create a way to visit India?

⟨?⟩ What's the fastest way to create a trip to Scotland?

⟨?⟩ What steps do I need to take today to get to Italy next year?

? Who do I know who loves to travel and would like to go with me on my next adventure?

? How can I go on four vacations a year and work less?

? Who will I meet who allows me to travel the world for free?

? What needs to happen to experience more travel?

? What adventures await me on my next trip?

Attitude

? What will surprise and delight me today?

? What is good and new?

? How much fun will I have today?

? What amazing person will I meet today?

? How fascinated will I be today with the world?

? What is beautiful today?

? How many things can I notice today that are inspiring?

? How can I be an inspiration to others?

? How can I walk in spirit and have compassion for all living things?

C Conclusion

The Magic Question is a simple technique that you can use every day, for the rest of your life. No matter how successful you become, there is always something more that you want. More love. More comfort. More time with your family. More happiness.

It is my sincere wish that you not only use this technique to attract more of the good things into your life, but you share this technique with your kids, your spouse, and your co-workers.

If all this technique does for people is to move them from the attitude of "problem frame" into the attitude of "solution frame", then I have succeeded. However, I feel the result will be much more than turning a pessimistic child into an optimistic, happy child. It can turn a struggling business into a cash-flow machine. It can turn a person in a dead-end job into an entrepreneur. It can turn a lonely person into a person in a loving, happy relationship.

It's all about asking the right question.

The most difficult part of writing this book was choosing and deleting the hours and hours of content which is available in my personal library of lectures, speeches, webinars, and notes which contain valuable tools and techniques.

I realize that the Magic Question is just one of many, many useful techniques and personal habits which can be used to transform your life, love, finances, and overall happiness.

If this is the first book of mine you have ever read, then I hope this is the start of a new relationship between you and me. I invite you to attend a live seminar or download some of my best-selling online training videos. I invite you to explore my other books. Many are sold on Amazon.com, and all the others are available at my company website.

http://bartbaggett.com/catalog/

While books are useful, there is no substitute for an immersive experience. If you can find a way to show up at a live event, I would love to shake your hand and hear about the wins you have had from this small book, The Magic Question. Then, I'd love to share with you the dozens of other techniques I've learned over the years to attract more prosperity, time, love, and freedom into my life. If you are an entrepreneur, thought leader, expert, or anyone who dreams of writing a book... do it. I have a number of resources and books, which can provide strategies and tools to make that dream a reality. I think everyone has a story to tell. Learn more at:

http://booksellingsecrets.com

Please take a moment and get on the early-notification list, which will guarantee you the first chance to secure a seat at my next event in your home country. Whether you are living in South Africa, India, Australia, the USA, Singapore, or any other country ... chances are you and I can meet one day soon.

Register for my email newsletter here:
http://bartbaggett.com

Until then... keep asking the right questions.

Bart Baggett

Los Angeles, California, USA

Other books and programs by Bart A. Baggett

Scan & Download

Success Secrets of the Rich and Happy: How to Design Your Life with Financial and Emotional Abundance
http://berichandhappy.com

Scan & Download

Unstoppable Confidence
http://unstoppableconfidence.net

Scan & Download

Unstoppable You
http://unstoppableyou.net/

Scan & Download

- **Neuro Audio Therapy Guided Meditation Downloads**
- **Fearless Living: Overcoming the Fear of Rejection**
- **Rapid Goal Achievement: Creating New Experiences and Designing Your Future while Rapidly Accomplishing Specific Goals**
  http://neuroaudiotherapy.com/

Scan & Download

How to Write a Best-Selling Book in 9.5 Hours (Free Download)

http://www.internationalauthorsassociation.org/books/writeabestsellerin9hours/

Scan & Download

The 7-Step Self-Publishing Formula

http://7stepselfpublishingformula.com

Scan & Download

The Perpetual Lead Machine
http://perpetualleadmachine.net/

Scan & Download

Facebook Marketing For Authors
http://fbmarketingforauthors.com

Scan & Download

How to Get 63 Authentic Amazon Reviews in 3 Days or Less: How to Market Your Book, Sell More Books on Kindle, Become a Best-Seller

http://booksellingsecrets.com/members/get-63-real-amazon-reviews-in-3-days

Scan & Download

How to Be a Highly Paid Hiring Consultant

http://myhandwriting.com/learn/market.html

Scan & Download

Unstoppable Confidence Guided Meditation Course
http://unstoppableconfidence.net

Scan & Download

Handwriting Analysis 101
http://handwritinguniversity.com/products/101/

Scan & Download

Learn Handwriting Analysis in 10 Minutes A Day (Free Download)

http://handwritinguniversity.com/10minutes/hwa-10min.html

Scan & Download

Change Your Handwriting, Change Your Life Workbook (Grapho-therapy journal for kids and adults)

http://myhandwriting.com/change/

Scan & Join now!

The Handwriting Analysis Certification Course
http://myhandwriting.com/learn/homestudy.html

Scan & Join now!

The 501 Handwriting Analysis Mastery Certification Course.
http://handwritinguniversity.com/products/mastery/